Wreaths
and Wall Flowers

Wreaths
and Wall Flowers

Gorgeous
Decorations
with Silk and
Dried Flowers

Ardith Beveridge, AIFD

**Creative Publishing
international**

Chanhassen, MN

Copyright 2006
Creative Publishing international
18705 Lake Drive East
Chanhassen, Minnesota 55317
1-800-328-3895
www.creativepub.com
All rights reserved

President/CEO: Ken Fund
Vice President/Retail Sales: Kevin Haas

Executive Editor: Alison Brown Cerier
Senior Editor: Linda Neubauer
Photo Stylist: Joanne Wawra
Creative Director: Brad Springer
Photo Art Director: Tim Himsel
Photographer: Steve Galvin
Production Manager: Laura Hokkanen

Cover Design: Lois Stanfield
Page Design and Layout: Lois Stanfield

Acknowledgments
Thanks to the following people and companies for their assistance and products:
John S. Maciejny, Koehler & Dramm, Smithers Oasis, Schuster's of Texas, Bella Creations,
Bloomsbury Market, Berwick Offray, Design Master, Sullivan's,
and Donna Stenberg of Flandreau Floral Shop

Library of Congress Cataloging-in-Publication Data

Beveridge, Ardith.
Wreaths and wall flowers : gorgeous decorations with silk and dried
flowers / by Ardith Beveridge.
p. cm.
ISBN 1-58923-253-4 (soft cover)
1. Wreaths. 2. Floral decorations. 3. Silk flower arrangement. 4.
Dried flower arrangement. I. Title.
SB449.5.W74B48 2006
745.92--dc22

2005026624

Printed in Singapore
10 9 8 7 6 5 4 3 2 1

Contents

6 **Creating Wreaths and Wall Designs**

Wreaths

15 Purple Berries and Blossoms

19 Contemporary Pinecones

23 Christmas Reds

27 A Different Christmas

31 Ranch Style

35 A Gardener's Wreath

39 Sweet Heart

43 Euro-Style Ring

47 Floral Reflections

51 Posh Peonies

55 Tumbled Pots

Wall Flowers

61 Wall Bouquets

65 Blooming Art

69 Purse of Poppies

73 Sea Monogram

77 Antiqued Basket of Roses

81 Woodland Cone

85 Floralscape

89 Floral Still Life

93 Wall Herb Garden

97 Sitting Pretty

101 Fall Welcome

105 Autumn Border

109 Copper Crescent

112 **About the Author**

Creating Wreaths and Wall Designs

Creating beautiful wreaths and wall flower designs for your home is easier than you might think, even if you have never designed with silk or dried flowers before. This book features twenty-four original projects for every room, every decorating style, and every season. There are complete materials lists and all the florals are identified in a separate photo. All the supplies are readily available in hobby and craft stores or from florist shops and online sources. Everything you need to know is taught in step-by-step instructions with photographs to show you the details.

You can approach a project in several ways. If you love every aspect of the design and want to create it exactly as pictured, simply follow the directions. If you have difficulty finding certain flowers or you want different colors, just substitute floral materials with similar shape and texture.

This part of the book will introduce you to the materials, tools, and techniques used throughout the projects.

The florals

The projects in this book use both faux flowers and dried natural floral materials. The following information will help you select and work with these materials.

Permanent botanicals

Faux florals are artificial flowers, but today's products are often so realistic that it's difficult to tell that they are not real. In the floral industry, faux florals are properly called "permanent botanicals." However, they are commonly referred to as "silk flowers," even though most are not made of silk but rather of polyester, latex, plastic, or a combination of materials.

Faux florals can be purchased in a wide range of qualities and prices, from inexpensive stems in solid colors to realistic stems with shading and veining. Most are made by machine. Hand-wrapped florals, at the higher end, are assembled by hand, though the parts may be made by machine. They may be parchment or fabric and are very realistic with wired stems and leaves. Some parchment and fabric flowers are dipped in latex to make them look more natural.

"Dried silk" flowers have a crinkled appearance with curled edges and resemble real dried flowers.

Faux florals are produced in four standard forms: the bush, the fantasy flower, botanical-like, and botanically correct.

Bush. A bush is a group of flowers and foliage on one stem, perhaps including accent flowers. A bush may include one type of flower or a combination. It is reasonably priced and easy to use whole or cut into individual stems.

Fantasy flowers. These flowers resemble real ones but have been designed to look different. For example, a flower might be made in a color in which it would not naturally exist, so that it can be used in a design where that color is needed.

Botanical-like. The florals are closer to the real thing, but the color, stem, foliage, or petal pattern has been changed to suit the desires of consumers. For example, a rose bush might have baby-blue flowers and have no dying flowers or broken stems.

Botanically correct. These are as close as possible to the real thing, though, of course, without the fragrance. The stem, pollen, leaf, root system, color, even branching structure are copied directly from nature. There is a remarkable degree of realism. Today's botanically correct florals look like, feel like, and are as flexible as real flowers. You may need to touch them to prove they are not fresh.

While botanically correct flowers and many botanical-like flowers are not inexpensive, they can be used as the focal point of an arrangement that includes inexpensive accent flowers. Top-quality florals are long lasting, so when you are tired of their first use, you can clean them and use them in other arrangements for added value.

Dried florals

Dried floral materials, available at craft stores, floral shops, and garden centers, are natural flowers, foliage, berries, pods, and grasses that have been dehydrated so they will last for a long time. They may have been dried in silica gel or preserved by freeze drying to retain their original shape, though their colors may have changed slightly. Foliage is often preserved in glycerin, which makes the leaves more flexible and easy to arrange without breaking.

You can also dry your own flowers and foliage. Bundle them in small groups with a rubber band wound around the stems. Hang them upside down in a dark, dry, warm area with constant airflow, such as the furnace room of your house. As the stems dry and shrink, the rubber band will tighten so the flowers won't fall. Constant airflow is important because the quicker the flowers dry, the more color they will retain.

Here are some tips for working with dried floral materials.

• Store delicate dried flowers in a cool area in a plastic bag to keep them soft and help them retain their color longer.

• The day before you want to work with the dried floral material, spray it with a mixture of five parts water and one part unscented fabric softener. Keep it in a sealed plastic bag overnight. This will moisten it, make it more pliable, and even enhance the color.

• Before working with heavy branches and vines, soak them in a five-to-one warm water/fabric softener mixture until they feel more pliable.

Mosses

Sheet moss. This is a natural, dried moss, also called sphagnum moss, used to cover foam and other mechanics of a design. It is packaged in sheets or layers that can be separated as they are needed. Apply glue with a glue gun and attach small pieces of moss at a time. To give life and color to sheet moss, soak it in water, squeeze to remove excess moisture, and place it flat between newspapers or paper towels.

Reindeer moss. Reindeer moss, so called because it is food for reindeer and caribou, is a ground lichen that grows in small clumps or mats. It is soft and spongy with hundreds of tiny branches that resemble ocean coral. Floral suppliers dye it in many colors for floral designing.

Display moss. Preserved moss is attached to a mesh fabric so it can be cut and shaped. It is available in widths of 16" or 24" (40.5 or 61 cm) in a 4-ft. (1.2 m) roll.

Choosing and combining colors

Color is the most important element of any floral design. After all, color is what flowers are all about. It's the first thing people notice. Also, more than any other element of a design, color interacts with the surroundings. Obviously, every flower does not come in every color, so your choices are limited to what is available. Even so, there are endless ways to combine colors, and experimenting with color is lots of fun. Here are some insights that will help you choose and combine colors effectively.

Warm colors (red, orange, yellow) tend to dominate other colors and may seem to project out from the design. Cool colors (green, blue, and violet) are calm and restful. They tend to blend into the background of a floral design.

Consider the ways the room's lighting will affect the colors. In dim light, colors look muted. The yellow glow of candlelight and incandescent lighting can turn pink to peach and baby blue to gray. Cool colors and blends tend to fade away in dim light.

Floral designers, like other artists, use the color wheel to show the relationship between colors and to help them choose colors that will work well together. On a color wheel, the twelve basic colors are arranged by how they are created and how they relate to each other.

Red, yellow, and blue are called primary colors, as they are not made from other colors. Orange, green, and violet are called secondary colors. Each is made by combining equal amounts of primary colors. Red plus yellow equals orange. Yellow plus blue equals green. Blue plus red equals violet. The two-name colors (red-orange, blue-violet) are called tertiary. They are made by combining one primary color and one secondary color in equal or unequal amounts.

(continued)

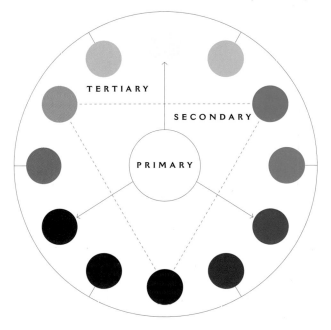

The color wheel can help you anticipate how certain combinations of colors will look in a wreath or wall flower design. Here are some of the possible color schemes.

Monochromatic. This is a design in one color. The design will be more interesting if the color is used in various intensities. In the example below, poppies in three shades of yellow-orange seem to be growing from a moss purse. In monochromatic arrangements, textures become more important.

Analogous. An analogous design uses colors that are next to each other on the color wheel. For example, the wall bouquets below use various shades of violet, red-violet, and blue-violet.

Complementary. This scheme uses florals in colors located on opposite sides of the color wheel—for example, yellow sunflowers and purple safflowers. The design will have strong contrast.

Materials and tools

You will want to set up a work space with tools and materials readily at hand. It is important to have the project hanging in front of you at eye level, while you work on it. A tabletop easel, purchased at an art supply store, works well for hanging your wreath or wall flower design. You could also hang it from a Peg-Board suspended behind a worktable.

Bases and containers

There are several kinds of bases on which you can design wreaths. They establish the size and shape of the wreath and provide a sturdy framework for anchoring floral materials. Metal forms, both round and square, and Styrofoam shapes in white, smooth green, and flocked green must be covered entirely by floral materials. Some bases, like grapevine and evergreen wreaths, are also a decorative part of the design and merely need to be embellished. Wreaths can also be designed on bases made of unusual materials, such as coils of rope, garden hose, or sturdy garlands wired together.

Other wall flowers need some sort of container for holding foam and flowers or a base for attaching

floral materials. There are lots of creative possibilities. Wall baskets and wall vases are great starting points for an endless variety of floral arrangements. Shelves are just waiting to be filled with interesting floral arrangements. Wall containers can be molded from chicken wire and display moss. You can design on foam-core board cutouts or use gesso-primed stretched artist canvases as backgrounds for floral art. Unexpected items like garden tools, small fences, and picture frames can be transformed with flowers.

Anchoring materials

Styrofoam is sold in white, greens, and browns in various sizes and shapes. It is used for anchoring thick-stemmed faux florals and materials on picks. When cutting Styrofoam with a knife, run the sharp blade edge into the side of an old candle before each cut, to help the knife cut smoothly and make less noise.

Dried floral foam is sold in blocks, sheets, wreaths, and shapes and available in greens, browns, and brights. Use it for designing with permanent botanicals and dried naturals. It grips stems securely and will not melt when glue or paint is applied.

Chicken wire is a net meshing that comes in gray or green. As a covering over dried floral foam, it provides stability in large designs. It can also be molded into a pocket shape and covered with display moss.

Adhesives and securing materials

Glue pan (1). A small electric skillet used to melt glue pellets.

Pan glue pellets (2). Nuggets or blocks of adhesive melted in a glue pan. Don't mix with glue sticks. Do not mix glues from different companies, as the chemical composition is different and the mixture may not adhere.

Paintbrush and honeystick (3). An inexpensive 2-inch paintbrush or a honeystick (page 11) used to apply glue to items too large or awkward to dip in the pan.

Small clay saucer (4). Placed in the glue pan to keep the brush and honeystick from resting on the bottom of the pan where they could burn.

Duct tape (5). One-sided, all-purpose tape, 2" (5 cm) wide, with a silver-gray surface on one side. Used to attach foam temporarily.

Anchor tape (6). Narrow tape on a roll in green, white, or clear; ½" (1.3 cm) width for large projects and ¼" (6 mm) width for small designs. Used for securing foam to the vessel.

Glue gun (7). Hot-glue tool used to secure foam and add trims. The high-temperature variety is best for faux floral work.

Glue sticks (8). For the glue gun; in white, clear, and glittered. This glue does not hold in cold temperatures, so don't use it on outdoor holiday designs. Choose the type recommended by the manufacturer of your glue gun.

Floral tape (9). Self-sealing wrapping tape in greens, browns, white, and rainbow colors. Used in floral design to wrap wires and lengthen stems.

Double-sided tape (10). Tape with adhesive on both sides; resists moisture and temperature extremes. Used for securing foam, candles, and accessory items like moss rocks.

Wood picks (11). Thin pieces of wood with a point on one end and a thin wire on the other, in green, brown, and natural. Used to secure objects like artificial fruit, to stabilize tall designs, and to extend stems. The 6" and 9" (15 and 23 cm) lengths will fill most of your needs.

Floral wire (12). Used to bind floral materials together and to lengthen stems that are too short for the design. Wires are 18" (46 cm) long and are sized in gauges from 16 to 28; the smaller the number, the thicker the wire. Wire in 24 gauge is versatile for faux floral designs.

Specialty wires

Barked wire (1) is a heavy-gauge wire that is wrapped in shades of brown or green raffia to look like a natural vine. It is used for supporting structures and binding heavy items to a base.

Bindwire (2) comes in a roll in natural and green colors. It is 26-gauge wire covered with raffia. Leave the outer plastic band on the roll and pull the wire from the inside to prevent the bindwire from tangling.

Aluminum craft wire (3) comes in several colors. Though relatively thick, it is very pliable and will hold the shape you give it.

Paddle wire (4) is 24-gauge green wire in a continuous roll, wrapped on a wooden or plastic paddle. The wire is unrolled from the paddle as it is needed, and cut only at the end of the step.

Bullion (5) is a very fine wire that comes in a coil, intended to be stretched into a long, kinky strand.

Tools

Knife (1). Large, sharp knife for cutting foam and a smaller knife for shaping foam. Choose a knife that feels comfortable in your hand. Sharpen after each use, and keep in a toolbox or other safe place.

Scissors (2). For cutting ribbon, foliage, fabrics, paper, or other items that do not contain metal. Sharpen regularly.

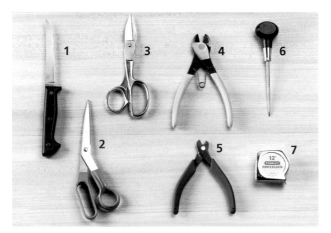

Shears (3). Very useful tool for cutting small wires and wired ribbon. Does not need to be sharpened.

Wire cutters (4). For cutting faux floral stems. Blades are shaped for cutting close to the stem.

Utility snips (5). For cutting thick stems, branches, thick wire, and chicken wire.

Awl (6). Sharp pointed metal rod for poking holes in firm materials.

Tape measure (7). For measuring foam size, stem lengths, and design proportions.

Techniques

Frequently used methods are explained here in more detail. Follow these techniques to complete your projects more efficiently and professionally.

Using a glue pan

A glue pan works at a lower and more variable temperature than a glue gun. Place the pan on a piece of hard plastic to protect your work surface. When you turn off the glue pan, you can keep the glue in it until next time. Set the temperature so that the glue is liquid but not smoking. There are two ways to apply the glue to materials.

Dipping. Floral foam and faux floral stems can be dipped into the glue pan before you secure them.

Brushing. When an object is too large or awkward to dip, you can transfer glue from the pan with a 2" (5 cm) paintbrush or a homemade honeystick. To make a honeystick, wrap a 12" (30.5 cm) chenille stem or pipe cleaner around 2" (5 cm) at the end of a 9" (23 cm) wood pick or any strong natural wood stick or branch (nothing plastic, cloth, or metal).

Using a glue gun

A glue gun is the best way to apply glue directly to a design—for example, to attach flowers or add trim. Heat the gun, place the tip where you want the glue, pull the trigger, and move the gun in a circular motion ending with an upward movement to break off the glue. The glue will be hot; if you aren't careful, you can get a nasty burn. Also, when the glue is hot, it will ooze out of the gun end at a touch of the trigger, so please be careful.

Cutting and attaching foam

1. Measure the opening of the container: side to side, front to back. Using a knife, cut the foam to fit the container. Then gently scrape a scrap of foam against the fitted piece to shape and smooth it.

2. Measure the height. This may be the same as the container depth or above or below the lip—check the instructions for the project. Place the foam into the container and mark where to cut with a marker. Remove and trim.

3. Dip the bottom of the foam into the glue pan. Place the foam into the container and press with your palm for a few seconds.

Preparing florals

When you buy a faux flower, it has been traveling a long way in a small box packed tightly with lots of other florals. So before you put it into a design, you need to fluff every flower and leaf. Bend and shape the stem. Open up the flowers and arrange the leaves in a natural way.

Many floral materials need to be reinforced so the flower heads won't separate from the stems later. This is particularly true when the blossom and leaves have been made separately and slipped onto the stem. Check the flower parts. If they aren't securely fastened, remove those parts. Then apply glue to the peg on the stem and replace the leaves or flowers. Allow the glue to set before you work with the material.

Cutting stems

Always cut a floral stem at a sharp angle using a wire cutter. The point makes it easier to insert the stem into foam. Often a faux floral stem includes several flowers as well as foliage. The instructions may say to cut the stem into pieces. Find a section in the main stem that has a long distance between smaller branches. Cut the main stem at an angle just above the lower branch. This will give the upper stem the length it needs. The flower at the end of the lower stem will top the newly cut stem.

If it is necessary to disguise the cut, touch up the area with paint to match the stem color. Often leaves can be bent or turned to hide a cut.

Inserting stems

1. Hold the stem in the place, at the height, and at the angle you think you'd like it. Move it around to be sure this is where you want it.

2. Push the stem into the spot you've chosen to the right depth. Put a finger on the stem just above the foam, and keep the finger there as you pull out the stem. Mark the spot.

3. Measure 2" to 3" (5 to 7.5 cm) below the mark. At this place, cut the stem at a sharp angle with a wire cutter. The point will pierce the foam; then as the stem gets larger, it will grip the foam securely.

4. Trim away any foliage or flowers that are in the 2" to 3" (5 to 7.5 cm) above the cut.

5. Place the stem into the desired place to check it once more before gluing. (As you gain experience, you will be able to skip this step.)

6. Dip the end of the stem into the glue pan. Immediately place the stem into the hole and hold it in place for a few seconds.

Wrapping floral wire

Floral wire is often wrapped with tape to make it easier to handle and less visible in the design.

1. Hold the end of the tape at the top of the wire. Twirl the wire in one hand while you wrap it with tape in spirals moving down the wire. Overlap the tape slightly and leave no gaps.

2. At the bottom of the wire, tear the tape. Seal the tape to the end of the wire by rolling the wire between your fingers.

Dividing a purchased wreath

When you buy a grapevine or honeysuckle vine wreath as a base for an arrangement, you can embellish it with floral materials just the way it is, but you can also separate it into two or three less dense wreaths and get more for your money! You can form the vines into wreaths of different sizes. You can even divide a grapevine wreath and a honeysuckle vine wreath and combine pieces of each to make several wreath bases that have interesting texture. Here's how to separate and work with vines. You may want to use a pair of light garden gloves when separating and working with the vines.

1. Wrap ten 18" (46 cm), 26-gauge wires with brown floral tape (left). Cut each of the taped wires

(continued)

into four parts. Place them in a vase or shallow container so they are easy to locate on the worktable. (They are the same color as the vine and could be swept away with loose branches.) Alternatively, use bindwire pieces.

2. Remove the vine that holds the wreath together. It is usually a larger vine that is wrapped around the entire wreath to secure and shape the enclosed vines. Set this aside.

3. Gently separate the wreath coil. Separate the vine into the amount and sizes of wreaths you have decided to make.

4. Gather two vine pieces in your hand. Wrap a piece of the taped wire or bindwire around the two vines; twist the wire tight against the vines. Leave the wire ends long so you will be able to add more vines later. Always secure only two vines together at a time; more than that will slip and not hold securely.

5. Wrap pieces of wire around the vines in several places to establish the size and shape of the wreath. Then add more vines to the wreath, twisting the existing wire tails around them to hold them in place. Continue until the wreath is as dense as you want it.

6. Coil the wire ends around a pencil to resemble natural vine tendrils.

Making a wire hanger

Prepare a wreath or other wall flower for hanging before you make the design. If the base is made of a material that can be easily bound with wire, such as grapevine, evergreen, or garlands, make a wire hanger.

1. Hold the wreath where you'd like it to hang. Tie a small piece of ribbon at the center of the design. If the design is large or long, you may want to attach hangers in two places.

2. Wrap a 10" (25.5 cm) piece of 22-gauge wire with floral tape (page 11) in a color that matches the design. For a large item, you may need heavier wire.

3. Bend the wire into a U shape. At the ribbon marker, run the ends through the base from back to front, catching two or more large vines near the inner edge of the wreath.

4. Twist the last 1" (2.5 cm) of the two wire ends together tightly. Pull the U tight, hiding the twisted ends in the wreath.

5. Twist the wire at the back of the wreath, forming a loop on your finger for hanging.

6. Mark the hanger with the ribbon. This will help you design the wall hanging in the right position and find the hanger when you are finished and are ready to position the piece on your wall.

Making a chenille stem hanger

For Styrofoam or foam-core bases, make the hanger from a chenille stem.

1. Cut a 4" (10 cm) piece of chenille stem (pipe cleaner) and bend it into a U shape.

2. Dip the ends of the chenille stem into the glue pan and insert them into the top center of the back of the wreath or wall design, ½" (1.3 cm) apart. Push the wires in at least ½" (1.3 cm). Allow the glue to set.

3. Bend the loop upward to form the hanger.

Wreaths

Purple Berries and Blossoms

This wreath is a tribute to the strength and character of the clematis vine, which wanders gracefully wherever it can attach itself, sending out curvy stems of leaves with broad blossoms that turn their faces to the sun. Purple glass berries catch the light and give a strong contrast in texture to the woodsy grapevine and delicate flowers. For added splash, a purple aluminum wire grabs your attention and draws your eye into all the interesting nooks.

Purple Berries and Blossoms

1. Lay the grapevine wreath and clematis flowers on newspapers in a well-ventilated area. Spray the wreath with glossy wood-tone color tool. Lightly spray the flower petals with the two flower dyes. Let them dry.

2. Wrap the 22-gauge wire with brown floral tape (page 11). Make a wire hanger at the top of the wreath, following the directions on page 12.

3. Wrap the 26-gauge wires with olive green floral tape and cut each wire into four equal pieces. Set them aside.

4. Bend the clematis garland into the shape of the grapevine wreath, letting it wander naturally with the ends meeting at the bottom. Secure the main stem of the garland to the grapevines

Florals
Oval grapevine wreath, 15" × 20"
  (38 × 51 cm)
One white or cream clematis garland, 24"
  (61 cm) long **(A)**
One clematis stem
One glass berry garland, 54" (137 cm) long **(B)**
Three stems wax flowers **(C)**

Tools and materials
Newspapers
Glossy wood-tone color tool
Lilac flower dye
Purple flower dye
One 18" (46 cm), 22-gauge wire
Brown floral tape
Four 18" (46 cm), 26-gauge wires
Olive green floral tape
Wire cutter
Glue pan or glue gun and glue
4 yd. (3.7 m) purple aluminum craft wire

in several places with wire pieces. Curl the ends of the wires to look like vine tendrils.

5   Bend the berry garland into the shape of the wreath, trailing it in and out of the clematis leaves with the ends meeting at the bottom. Secure the main stem of the garland to the grapevines in several places with wire. Hang the wreath over your work surface.

6   Cut the flowers from the clematis stem, leaving the stems as long as possible. Glue them into the wreath wherever more flowers are needed. Make sure the stems all go in the same direction as the garlands.

7   Cut the wax flower stems into three parts each. Dip the ends in glue and tuck them into the grapevine here and there, turning the stems in the same direction as the garlands.

8   Secure one end of the aluminum wire deep into the grapevines. Bend and twist the wire all around the wreath, creating a dynamic, flowing line. Secure the other end deep into the wreath.

4

8

Ardith suggests

When you design a wreath, pay attention to all the surfaces, including the inner ring. Let some of the flowers and foliage trail off the edges and into the center the way they would grow naturally. This way, the wreath won't look like it has a big hole in the middle—the look is more pleasing and artistic.

Contemporary Pinecones

Most pinecone wreaths have a lodge-style look, but this one is dramatic and contemporary. Pinecones of different sizes radiate outward, and a tangle of beaded berries fills the center. Wide-striped satin ribbon tied up in a bow adds a dressy touch. This wreath can be displayed from early fall into early spring. If you want to give it a holiday look, simply change the ribbon.

Contemporary Pinecones

1   Spread newspapers over the work surface. Trace the inner and outer edges of the wreath base on the newspaper.

2   Cut or tear sheet moss into pieces and lay them facedown over the traced lines. Place the wreath base faceup over the moss. Cover the front of the wreath base with moss. Wrap 22-gauge paddle wire around the wreath base to hold the moss in place.

3   Wrap the 20-gauge wire with floral tape (page 11). Make a wire hanger at the top of the wreath, following the directions on page 12.

4   Cut six 12" (30.5 cm) pieces of bindwire. Arrange the six sugar pinecones on the wreath

Florals
Sheet moss
Six large sugar pinecones **(A)**
18 medium pinecones **(B)**
Five stems green beaded berries,
    24" (61 cm) long **(C)**

Tools and materials
Newspaper
Green wire wreath base,
    18" (46 cm) diameter
Green 22-gauge paddle wire
One 18" (46 cm), 20-gauge wire
Brown floral tape
Scrap of ribbon, for marking hanger
Brown bindwire
Wire cutter
Needle-nose pliers
Glossy wood-tone color tool
4 yd. (3.7 m) satin ribbon,
    3" (77 mm) wide

frame with the narrow ends out, leaving a center space about 5" (12.7 cm) wide. Wrap a piece of bindwire around each pinecone and through the wreath base; twist the ends together on the back of the wreath, holding the pinecone firmly in place.

5 Cut 18 pieces of bindwire, each 9" (23 cm) long. Wire a medium pinecone to the wreath between a pair of large pinecones, snugging the base into the center of the wreath as close as you can. Then wire a medium pinecone, narrow end in, to each side of it. Repeat between each pair of large pinecones.

6 Lay the wreath on newspapers in a well-ventilated area. Spray the pinecones with glossy wood-tone color tool. Let it dry.

4

7 Gather the berry stems together and wrap them around your hand. Tuck the ring of stems into the center of the wreath. Spread out the berries into a tangled mound. Trail some of the stems among the bases of the pinecones to keep the mound in place.

8 Tie wide ribbon into a bow with long tails. Tack the bow to the wall above the wreath, and let the tails drape down behind the sides of the wreath.

Ardith suggests

If you want to use pinecones you have found, first swish them around in a sink of warm water to dislodge any insects and soil. Lay them on newspapers to dry. Then place them in an oven set at 200°F (95°C) for 20 to 30 minutes. Your pinecones will be sanitized and the heat will activate the resin to release a wonderful pine aroma.

Christmas Reds

Nothing says Christmas like an evergreen wreath with bright red accents. In this design, lavishly ruffled roses on one side balance a generous peppering of berries on the other. Clusters of shiny metallic ornaments and a wandering metallic mesh make it sparkle. And everything is red! Nothing is glued into this wreath, so you can change the theme each year and reuse all the pieces.

Christmas Reds

1   Fluff the wreath into a natural shape by pulling out and twisting each branch.

2   Wrap the 22-gauge wire with floral tape (page 11). Make a wire hanger at the top of the wreath, following the directions on page 12.

Ardith suggests

Faux evergreens can scratch and dry out your hands and fingernails, so wear a pair of garden gloves when you work with them.

Florals

One mixed evergreens wreath with pinecones, 20" (51 cm) diameter **(A)**

One red berry garland, 2 yd. (1.85 m) long **(B)**

Three large open red roses with foliage **(C)**

Tools and materials

One 18" (46 cm), 22-gauge wire

Brown floral tape

Wire cutter

24 red holiday balls on wire stems, 35 mm diameter **(D)**

5 yd. (4.6 m) red metallic mini floral wrapper **(E)**

3 Bend the berry garland in half, shape it into a crescent, and lay it over the right side of the wreath. Secure the garland to the wreath in several places by twisting an evergreen branch around the main stem of the garland. Spread out the berry stems and tuck them in and out of the evergreen branches.

4 Remove the rose blossoms and foliage from the stems, leaving the stems 2" (5 cm) long. Tuck the roses into the wreath on the left side; one at the bottom, one at the upper left, and the other one between them. Secure them by twisting evergreen branches around the rose stems. Add rose foliage around the roses, securing them in the same way.

3

5 Twist the wire stems of three holiday balls together from the base to the ends. Repeat to make eight clusters. Insert the ball clusters into the wreath, spacing them evenly. Secure them by twisting evergreen branches around the wire stems.

6 Form a large loop in the mini floral wrapper about 18" (46 cm) from the end. Secure the loop to the wreath at the bottom, just to the right of the center, by twisting evergreen branches over it. Loosely trail the mini floral wrapper around the wreath clockwise, tucking it in and out of the branches. Form another loop near the first one to resemble a bow, and secure it with an evergreen branch. Trim the tail to the desired length.

5

A Different Christmas

This elegant, contemporary wreath has an unusual shape and materials for a Christmas wreath. Fresh magnolia leaves are blended with dried salal leaves to form the base for the parchment roses and gold ball ornaments. Fresh magnolia leaves are inserted with the underside facing out because they dry to a natural golden brown that adds color and texture to the wreath. A rich, gold satin ribbon, tied in a prim Dior bow, only appears to support the wreath; there are wire hangers at the upper corners.

A Different Christmas

1 Cut the wires from the roses. Lay the salal wreath and parchment roses on newspapers in a well-ventilated area. Lightly spray them with the flower dye. Let them dry.

2 Wrap the 22-gauge wires with floral tape (page 11). Make a wire hanger at each upper corner of the wreath, following the directions on page 12. Hang the wreath over your work surface.

3 Cut the magnolia leaves from the branch. Glue them among the salal leaves here and there with the undersides facing outward. All the leaves should point in the same direction as the foliage on the premade wreath.

4 Glue the large roses into the wreath, placing one in the upper left corner near the inner edge, one in the center of the upper right corner, one in the center bottom, and one in the center of the lower left corner.

Florals
Four large ivory parchment roses (A)
Nine small ivory parchment roses (B)
One square dried salal wreath,
    14" (35.5 cm) wide (C)
One branch fresh magnolia foliage (D)

Tools and materials
Wire cutter
Newspaper
Brown flower dye
Two 18" (46 cm), 22-gauge wires
Brown floral tape
Glue pan or glue gun and glue
Five antique gold ornaments,
    2¼" (6 cm) diameter
4 yd. (3.7 m) antique gold double-face
    wired ribbon, 1½" (39 mm) wide
Ribbon scissors
Straight pins
Two pushpins

5 Glue the ornaments into the wreath, placing one in the upper left corner above and to the left of the rose, one in the center of the top near the inner edge, one near the upper right corner below and to the right of the rose, one in the lower right corner near the inner edge, and one in the lower left corner near the outer edge.

6 Glue the small roses into the wreath, placing three in the center top, one just below the center of the right side near the outer edge, two in the lower right corner on either side of the ornament, one in the center bottom under the large rose, one in the lower left corner above and to the right of the large rose, and one in the center of the left side near the inner edge.

7 Cut pieces of ribbon 14", 3", and 21" (35.5, 7.5, and 53.5 cm) long. To make a Dior bow, place the 14" length on the work surface and fold in the ends so they overlap slightly in the center; glue in place. Wrap the 3" piece around the center, keeping the bow center flat; glue the ends in place on the back. Fold the 21" piece so one tail is longer than the other; cut inverted Vs in the ribbon ends. Using pins or glue, form a loop 2" (5 cm) from the end of each tail. Glue the tails to the back of the bow.

8 Cut a piece of ribbon 24" (61 cm) long. Glue the ends deep into the wreath at the upper corners. Fold the ribbon diagonally in the center and glue the Dior bow over the fold.

9 Cut the remaining ribbon in half and form each piece into three loops and a tail. Cut inverted V's in the tails. Glue one under the rose in the upper left corner; glue the other under the ornament in the lower right corner.

10 Hang the wreath by the wire hangers at the corners. Tack the Dior bow in place above the wreath, using two pushpins hidden inside the bow loops.

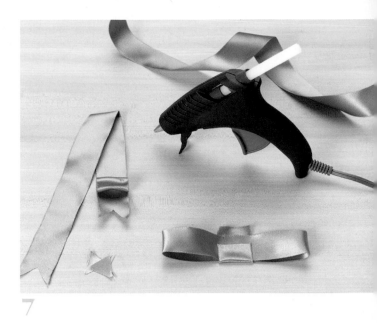

7

9

Ardith suggests

Change the look by hanging the wreath as a diamond instead of a square. Attach the ribbons to the upper sides and let them drape through the opening.

Ranch Style

This wreath reminds me of the prairies and ranches in South Dakota where I grew up. The rope and camphor vine have a wonderful rugged texture, and the thistles, pods, and grass heads are rustic and no-frills. Pheasant feathers add a rural touch. Some sunny, carefree cosmos soften the look a bit and add color. This design would bring western style to a den or family room.

Ranch Style

1. Wrap the two lengths of rope loosely around each other and coil them into four or five loops ranging from 10" to 16" (25.5 to 40.5 cm) in diameter. Join them tightly together at the top with two wraps of anchor tape.

2. Form the camphor vine into four or five loops about the size of the larger rope loops. Join them tightly to the rope at the top with several wraps of anchor tape.

3. Wrap the 22-gauge wire with floral tape (page 11). Make a wire hanger at the top of the wreath, following the directions on page 12. Hang the wreath over your work surface.

4. Curve the beautyberry sprays. Glue the stem ends deep into the rope coils, one cascading to the right over the outside of the rope and

Florals
One dried camphor vine **(A)**
Two sprays beautyberry with yellow berries **(B)**
Two stems cosmos, each with five flowers and buds **(C)**
One branch thistle with 12 stems **(D)**
One bunch natural grass with three stems **(E)**
Five to seven pheasant feathers **(F)**
Nine assorted pods **(G)**

Tools and materials
3 yd. (2.75 m) hemp rope, ½" (1.3 cm) diameter
3 yd. (2.75 m) hemp rope, ¼" (6 mm) diameter
Green anchor tape
One 18" (46 cm), 22-gauge wire
Brown floral tape
Wire cutter
Glue pan or glue gun and glue
Branch cutter

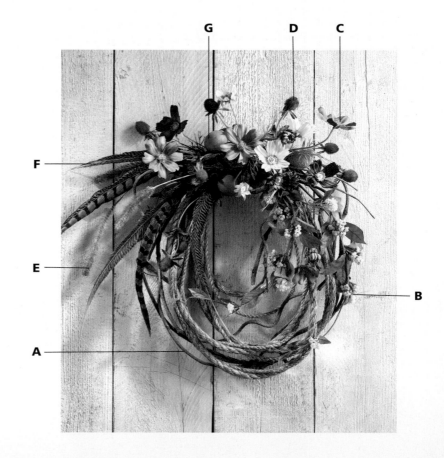

the other cascading to the right and into the center of the wreath.

5 Cut the cosmos flowers, thistles, and grass heads into individual stems. Sort them into groups.

6 Cut the cosmos stems at various lengths and glue them into the top of the wreath. Bend the stems gracefully and turn the heads upward for a natural look. Drape one or two down to the right.

7 Cut the thistle stems at various lengths. Glue them into the top of the wreath, with most of them extending to the left, a few upward, and two to the right.

8 Bend the three grass stems slightly and glue them into the wreath, extending toward the left.

9

9 Carefully insert the pheasant feathers, arcing out over the left side of the wreath. If your feathers are straight, curve them by gently creasing the back of the spine every 1/8" (3 mm) with the dull edge of a knife, working from the thick end to the tip.

10 Glue the pods in different positions over and near the wrapped area at the top of the wreath.

Ardith suggests

Asymmetry is a great way to create interest. When you're making a wreath, avoid the urge to space flowers equally or to make one side of your wreath mirror the other side. The feathers and stems on this wreath all radiate from a point that is just slightly off center. Putting all the feathers on one side and the leafy berry vines on the other makes this wreath more interesting, yet there is still overall balance and harmony.

33

A Gardener's Wreath

Picture this wreath on the sunny wall of a porch or sunroom, a flowerbed or vegetable garden somewhere nearby. This design is just one example of all the creative possibilities for wreath bases and novelty accents. With the simple addition of grapevine garland and some very realistic cherry tomatoes, tools from the hardware store can be transformed into home décor.

A Gardener's Wreath

1   Coil the hose into four or five loops ranging from 12" to 18" (30.5 to 46 cm) in diameter, with one end to the right at the top and the other end at the bottom. Join them tightly together at the top with several wraps of anchor tape.

2   Wrap the 22-gauge wire with floral tape (page 11). Make a wire hanger at the top of the wreath, following the directions on page 12. Hang the wreath over your work surface.

3   Cut the grapevine garland in half and lay one length over the other. Using the anchor tape, secure the garland to the wreath with one-fourth of the garland to the right and the rest draping down over the hose to the left.

Florals
One grapevine garland, 2 yd. (1.85 m) long **(A)**
One tomato plant **(B)**

Tools and materials
Garden hose, 5 yd. (4.6 m) long
Green anchor tape, ½" (1.3 cm) wide
One 18" (46 cm), 22-gauge wire
Green floral tape
Bundle of green raffia **(C)**
Garden trowel and rake
Garden gloves
Glue pan or glue gun and glue
Ribbon scissors

4   Tie two or three lengths of raffia to the handle of each garden tool. Dangle the tools down into the center of the wreath, one hanging lower than the other. Tie the raffia ends over the anchor tape at the top of the wreath. Leave the raffia tails long.

5   Gather the gloves at the wrist and wrap them tightly together with raffia. Then wire them over the garland and around the hose at the top of the wreath, with the fingers hanging down into the center of the wreath.

6   Cut the tomato plant apart, separating the foliage and fruit stems. Glue the pieces to the raffia behind the gloves, allowing some to drape down on each side.

7   Make a large bow with several strands of raffia. Tie the bow around the gloves, covering the wire, and then to the top of the wreath. Knot some of the raffia tails together at the bottom of the wreath. The others can trail off to the sides.

Ardith suggests

This wreath would make a great house-warming gift. The wreath is easy to take apart later, so the recipient can actually use the garden tools, gloves, and hose.

3

5

Sweet Heart

This charming heart-shaped wreath could welcome a newborn home to the nursery or decorate a little girl's room. With its fluffy white carnations and tufts of tulle, it could even be used as a wedding decoration. Simply change the color of the ribbons and roses to suit the room or occasion.

Sweet Heart

1 In the top center of the heart, make a hanger with the chenille stem, following the directions on page 12. Allow the glue to set.

2 Touch a drop of glue to the back of the wreath form and place the end of the white satin ribbon over it; secure with a straight pin. Then wrap the heart tightly with ribbon, overlapping the ribbon edges slightly with each wrap. Secure with occasional touches of glue on the back of the heart. Wrap the ribbon around and through the hanger. Secure the finishing end with a drop of glue and a straight pin.

3 Twist the wire stems of five miniature roses together from the base to the ends. Repeat to make four clusters of five roses and one cluster of four roses. Trim the twisted stems to 1" (2.5 cm). Cut the stems of the remaining roses to 1" (2.5 cm). Set the roses aside.

Florals
Three nosegays miniature paper roses with leaves (12 flowers each), in color of choice **(A)**
12 white carnations **(B)**

Tools and materials
One open white Styrofoam heart, 12" (30.5 cm) wide
One white chenille stem
Glue gun and glue
8 yd. (7.35 m) white satin ribbon, 1½" (39 mm) wide
Ribbon scissors
Three straight pins
Wire cutter
7¼ yd. (6.65 m) satin ribbon, ⅛" (3 mm) wide, in color of choice
Twelve 6" (15 cm) squares white tulle

A ———

——— B

2

3

4 Cut the narrow ribbon into 12 pieces, 18" (46 cm) long. Tie a simple shoelace bow in the center of each piece, leaving long tails. Set them aside.

5 Cut a carnation from its stem. Remove the calyx (the green part on the underside of the blossom). Glue the petals together at the bases with the glue gun, making sure the flower will not come apart. Repeat for each carnation. Set them aside.

Ardith suggests

Styrofoam also comes in other shapes, including rings of various sizes that can be decorated for wreaths or wall flowers. If you don't find a shape you like, you can cut one from a sheet of Styrofoam, using a knife or coping saw. Smooth the cut edges by rubbing them with a scrap of Styrofoam.

6 Fold a tulle square in half and in half again. Holding the tulle at the folded point, trim the cut edges into a curve. The tulle will unfold into a butterfly shape. Repeat for each tulle square. Set them aside.

7 Hang the wreath over your work surface Glue a carnation to the top point and one to the bottom point of the wreath front, using a generous amount of hot glue. Then glue the remaining carnations, evenly spaced, on each side.

8 Glue a single rose into the center of each carnation. Then glue the rose clusters here and there around the wreath.

9 Gather the center of a tulle butterfly in your fingers, forming a little tuft. Place a drop of glue on the wreath base between two carnations and tuck the tuft into the glue. Repeat, gluing tufts of tulle here and there around the wreath.

10 Glue the ribbon bows here and there around the wreath, letting the tails hang free.

Euro-Style Ring

Simplicity can be very soothing. This slender white wreath of gypsophila can be hung in a room that is busy with colorful patterns and textures to give the eye a resting place. Long ivory ribbons draping from the center top have a calming effect and are punctuated with small blossoms in a silver boutonniere cone. I chose red roses for high contrast, but you can use any bright flower or substitute a keepsake brooch.

Euro-Style Ring

1 Mix together five parts water and one part unscented fabric softener in a spray bottle. Spray the gypsophila with the mixture and put it in a large plastic bag for a couple of hours.

2 Lay the wreath frame on newspapers in a well-ventilated area. Spray the frame on both sides alternately with the flower dye and the white color tool until the frame is nearly white. Let the frame dry.

3 Arrange half the package of white sisal in a circle on the work surface and lay the wreath frame over it. Then spread the remaining sisal evenly over the top of the wreath frame.

Florals
Two packages dried glycerized
    gypsophila **(A)**
One package white sisal
One or two red roses (or flower
    of choice) **(B)**

Tools and materials
Fabric softener and water spray bottle
Large plastic bag
One wire wreath frame, 18"
    (46 cm) diameter
Newspaper
White flower dye
White color tool
One roll silver bullion wire
Wire cutter
One white chenille stem
Glue gun and clear glue
2½ yd. (2.3 m) each of four or five
    ivory ribbons in different styles
    and widths
Silver flower cone pin
Ribbon scissors

4   Wrap the wreath frame with the silver bullion wire, catching the sisal under the wire and wrapping the wire randomly. Continue until the sisal is secure and the frame has a metallic sparkle. Tie off the wire.

5   Make a hanger with the chenille stem, following the directions for a wire hanger on page 12. Allow the glue to set. Hang the wreath over your work surface.

6   Remove the gypsophila from the plastic bag. Cut the branches into smaller pieces with 1" to 2" (2.5 to 5 cm) stems, and arrange them on the work surface in 20 small groups.

7   Using the hot-glue gun, place some glue in a spot at the bottom of the wreath; then glue a cluster of gypsophila stems in place. Repeat around the wreath.

8   Gather all the ribbons together and fold them in half over the top of the wreath. Insert one or two flowers into the cone pin, and fasten the cone pin through the ribbon layers to keep the ribbons in place. Trim the ribbon ends at different lengths and angles as desired.

4

7

Ardith suggests

When gluing the gypsophila to the wreath, begin at the bottom. Then rotate the wreath a little and repeat, so you are always working at the bottom. Continue around until the wreath is complete. This will keep hot glue from dripping down into the finished area of the wreath.

Floral
Reflections

Give a tired mirror a new life with a wreath of permanent botanicals. Here white flowers in various sizes and bunches of green berries rest in a bed of magnolia leaves covering the frame of an oval mirror. Flowers and foliage spilling into the center of the wreath are reflected in the mirror. Adorned this way, the mirror becomes a decorative accent that can brighten an entrance or hallway.

Floral Reflections

1 Wash and dry the mirror. Place it faceup on the work surface. Cut about 25 pieces of bindwire, each 6" (15 cm) long, and set them aside.

2 Curve the magnolia garland counterclockwise over the mirror frame. Wire the garland stems together to hold the shape, using the bindwire.

3 Curve the stems of the magnolia flowers counterclockwise over the garland and mirror frame, overlapping them so the flowers are spaced fairly evenly; one just left of the center top, one just left of the center bottom, and one on the right side. Wire the flower heads to the stems and magnolia garland beneath them. Then wire the stems together in several more places. The wires in the magnolia stems form the wreath base.

Florals
One magnolia garland, 72" (183 cm) long **(A)**
Three large magnolia flowers with stems and foliage **(B)**
Three stems white freesia, each with three flowers **(C)**
Two stems white alstroemeria, each with five flowers **(D)**
Three stems sweet peas, each with three flowers **(E)**
Two stems lisianthus, each with two flowers and a bud **(F)**
Three bunches green berries, each with seven branches **(G)**

Tools and materials
Oval mirror in a wooden frame, 22" × 18" (56 × 46 cm)
Green bindwire
Wire cutter

3

9

4 Divide each freesia stem into two parts. Wire them into the wreath at evenly spaced intervals, with the stems running counterclockwise.

5 Curl and twist the alstroemeria stems. Wire them into the wreath to the right of the top magnolia.

6 Curl and twist the sweet pea stems. Wire them into the wreath at three evenly spaced places where more texture is needed.

Ardith suggests

Attaching the mirror this way won't damage the mirror or the frame. If you don't care about that, you can staple across the garland stems in several places into the wooden frame or use generous amounts of hot glue.

7 Curve the lisianthus stems to the shape of the mirror frame. Wire them to the magnolia stems and garland so the flowers of one stem are at the lower right and the flowers of the other stem are at the upper left.

8 Curve the berry stems to the shape of the mirror frame. Wire them to the wreath; one bunch of berries on the right side and the other two bunches on the left.

9 Cut a piece of bindwire 6" (15 cm) longer than the mirror measurement from top to bottom. Cut another piece 6" (15 cm) longer than the mirror measurement from side to side. Cut two pieces 6" (15 cm) longer than the diagonal measurement. Slide the wires under the mirror in these positions with equal lengths extending around the wreath. (If the mirror has a wire for hanging, be sure the bindwires go through it.) Bring the wires to the front and secure them tightly around the main stems in the wreath.

Posh Peonies

This wreath combines showy blossoms of peonies with lush clusters of green grapes. The combination is unexpected, and the contrast in color and texture is very pleasing. With a setting of magnolia—both the leaves and twisting vines—the overall look is both upscale and very pretty.

Posh Peonies

1 Wrap the wires with floral tape (page 11) and cut each into four equal pieces. Bend the wires into U shapes and set them aside, sorted by gauge.

2 Remove the flowers and foliage from the peony stems and arrange the flowers, foliage, and stems in separate groups on the work surface. All the pieces will be used in the wreath.

3 Glue the peony leaves to the wreath base. Turn the leaves in all directions and cover as much of the base as possible.

4 Make a hanger with the chenille stem, following the directions on page 12. Allow the glue to set.

5 Remove some of the tendrils from the magnolia garland and set them aside. Shape the garland into a wavy ring and lay it over the wreath base. Dip the ends of a bent 20-gauge wire

Florals
Eight peony stems with foliage **(A)**
One magnolia garland, 4½ ft. (1.4 m) long **(B)**
Three large grape clusters **(C)**

Tools and materials
Five 18" (46 cm), 20-gauge wires
Three 18" (46 cm), 22-gauge wires
Brown floral tape
Wire cutter
Green foam wreath base, 16" (40.5 cm) diameter
Glue pan or glue gun and glue
One green chenille stem

3

5

7

from step 1 into the glue. Straddle a garland stem with the wire and insert the wire ends into the wreath base. Repeat around the wreath with the remaining wires, securing the garland to the base.

6 Glue the flower heads into the wreath in and around the leaves and stems of the garland. Vary the placement and spacing for a natural look. Hang the wreath over your work surface.

7 Cut each grape cluster into three pieces. Tuck the grapes into the wreath between the peonies. Vary the placement and spacing for a natural look. Secure them with 22-gauge wires from step 1, using the same technique used for securing the garland.

8 Wrap a peony stem around your arm a few times and then remove it and uncoil it so it curves in gentle arcs. Dip the stem ends into the glue; insert one end into the wreath base. Trail the stem naturally among the leaves, peonies, and grapes and then insert the other end into the wreath base. Repeat with the remaining stems, adding them at various positions around the wreath to create a feeling of motion.

9 Add the reserved garland tendrils here and there around the wreath, following the technique in step 8.

Ardith suggests

In addition to, or in place of, the grape clusters, glue small green apples or limes among the magnolia leaves of your wreath. Faux fruits are very lightweight, so a quick dip in the glue pan is enough to hold them in place.

Tumbled Pots

This is a whimsical garden wreath of terra-cotta pots nestled in grapevine garland. Flowers and berries with different colors and textures spill from the pots in all directions. Though the design seems unstructured, balance is created by using pots in several sizes. Hang this wreath in a kitchen or sun-room to bring the outdoors inside.

Tumbled Pots

1 Wrap the 20-gauge wire with floral tape (page 11). Make a wire hanger at the top of the wreath, following the directions on page 12.

2 Lay the grapevine garland over the wreath, tucking it in and out of the wreath vines to hold it in place temporarily. The garland will be caught in place when the pots are wired onto the wreath.

3 Cut three pieces of bindwire 24" (61 cm) long, three pieces 18" (46 cm) long, three pieces 12" (30.5 cm) long, and 18 pieces 9" (23 cm) long.

4 Thread one of the longest wires into one of the largest pots, out the drain hole, and back to the top. Position the pot on the wreath near

Florals
One grapevine wreath, 18" (46 cm) diameter
One grapevine garland, 3 ft. (0.92 m) long **(A)**
Sheet moss or reindeer moss
One bunch wax flowers with seven stems **(B)**
One stem alstroemeria with five blossoms **(C)**
One miniature rose spray with eight blossoms
    and several buds **(D)**
One bunch lavender with seven stems **(E)**
One bunch hypericum with five stems **(F)**
Green sisal **(G)**

Tools and materials
One 18" (46 cm), 20-gauge wire
Brown floral tape
Roll of natural bindwire
Wire cutter
Three clay pots, 4¼" (10.8 cm) diameter
Three clay pots, 3" (7.5 cm) diameter
Three clay pots, 2¼" (6 cm) diameter
Three clay pots, 1¾" (4.5 cm) diameter
Three clay pots, 1¼" (3.2 cm) diameter
One block dry floral foam
Knife
Glue pan or glue gun and glue
Bundle of natural raffia

the top, facing left and dipping into the wreath center. Thread the bindwire through some strong wreath vines near the top of the pot and twist the ends tightly together. Slip one of the shortest bindwires over the first wire near the bottom of the pot. Thread this wire through some strong vines near the bottom of the pot and twist the ends tightly together, snugging the pot to the wreath. Coil the bindwire ends to resemble tendrils.

5   Add the other two large pots to the wreath, wiring them as in step 4. Catch the garland in place with some of the wires. Place one on the left facing up and the other to the right of the bottom, facing up and right, as in the photo on page 54. Secure the 3" (7.5 cm) pots: one

upside down on the left under the larger pot, one right side up on the right, and the other on the outer edge at the top, facing right.

6   Add the rest of the pots, one size at a time, wiring them as in step 4. Tip them in different directions and vary the locations to include all areas of the wreath. Catch the garland in place with some of the wires. Hang the wreath over your work surface. Make sure all the pots are wired securely.

7   Cut the foam block into even thirds and cut each piece in half. Glue a one-sixth block into the bottom of each of the largest pots. Cut the three remaining one-sixth pieces in half. Glue a one-twelfth piece into the bottom of each of the 3" (7.5 cm) pots. Cut the three remaining one-twelfth pieces in half and glue one piece into the bottom of each 2¼" (6 cm) pot. Continue dividing the foam and gluing small pieces into each pot.

(continued)

8

8 Glue a patch of sheet moss or reindeer moss into each pot to cover the foam.

9 Cut the flowers apart into individual stems 4" to 6" (10 to 15 cm) long; arrange them in groups of each kind.

10 Insert the wax flowers into the largest pot at the top of the wreath, letting them spill naturally over the pot edge. Insert the alstroemeria blossoms and foliage into the large pot near the bottom. Reserve three rose blossoms; insert the rest of the roses into the large pot on the left side of the wreath.

11 Insert the remaining three roses into the 3" (7.5 cm) pot on the right. Reserve a few lavender stems; insert the rest of the lavender into the upside-down 3" (7.5 cm) pot. Reserve a few hypericum stems; insert the rest of the hypericum into the 3" (7.5 cm) pot at the top of the wreath. Insert the reserved stems into the remaining small pots. Some pots can be left empty.

12 Cut ten 3-yd. (2.75 m) lengths of raffia and hold them together; form a bow in the center. Tie the bow with another piece of raffia, and tie the bow to the top of the wreath over the largest pot. Let the raffia streamers loop around the pots and foliage. Add more raffia loops behind the pots in the lower left inner edge.

13 Spread the green sisal in your hands and stretch it irregularly over the wreath, around the pots.

Ardith suggests

Green sisal, spread thinly over the surface of a wreath or other wall design, adds texture, softens the hard edges of stems and vines, and veils the wires and glue that hold the pieces in place.

Wall Flowers

Wall Bouquets

Glass wall vases make it easy to put bouquets of flowers right on your wall. In this design, the stems are swaddled in floral wrapper to bring color down into the clear vases. Aluminum craft wire adds shine as it coils around the bouquets and down over the vases. You can mount the vases one above the other on a narrow wall or side by side at staggered heights. They can also be used like sconces on either side of a mirror in an entry or above a dresser.

Wall Bouquets

1 Cut the dahlia and larkspur into individual stems. Sort them in two groups, one for each vase.

2 Hold a mixed flower bush in your hand. Add the individual dahlia and larkspur stems so they rise above the bush in a pleasing arrangement. Wrap the stems together with anchor tape just below the lowest flowers.

3 Hold the bouquet against the vase so the lowest flowers will drape out over the vase lip. Mark where the stems should be cut. Using a wire cutter, cut the stems.

Florals
Two stems dahlia, each with two
    flowers and a bud **(A)**
Two stems larkspur, each with
    two flowers **(B)**
Two mixed white bushes, each with
    multiple flowers and foliage **(C)**

Tools and materials
Green anchor tape, ¼" (6 mm) wide
Two glass wall vases
Wire cutter
Floral wrapper **(E)**
2 yd. (1.85 m) aluminum craft
    wire **(D)**

4 Cut a square of floral wrapper about 10" (25.5 cm) larger than twice the depth of the vase. Place the ends of the stems into the center of the square and gather the floral wrapper up around them. Wind aluminum wire several times around the wrapped stems, just under the blossoms.

5 Insert the bouquet into the vase. Coil aluminum wire around the vase and up into the bouquet.

4

Ardith suggests

Don't try to make your bouquets identical. Use the same flowers, but arrange them differently to make them more interesting.

Blooming Art

Here, florals are turned into a piece of "modern art." Pick nine of one kind of bright flower and showcase them in water tubes along three pieces of artist canvas. You don't have to be an artist to paint a couple of bold, wavy strokes; just be brave and grab a brush. Hang your interpretive floral art in a hallway or other horizontal space where you want to make a bold statement.

Blooming Art

1. Lay the canvases in a row on your work surface, with edges touching. Blend the paint colors as desired. Paint two long wavy strokes across all three canvases. Let the paint dry. Mark the backs of the canvases 1, 2, and 3, to keep them in order.

2. Mark a pencil line across the back of each canvas 4" (10 cm) from the top. Then mark a point at the center of the line and points 2½" (6.5 cm) to each side.

3. Punch two holes ½" (1.3 cm) apart at each marked point, using an awl.

4. Mark a pencil line on a water tube 2" (5 cm) below the lip. Place a small amount of glue on the tube near the top and wrap the tube with raffia from the lip to the mark. Glue the end to the back of the tube. Repeat for each tube.

Florals
Nine mini gerbera daisies **(A)**

Tools and materials
Three gesso-primed stretched canvases,
    9" × 12" (23 × 30.5 cm)
Acrylic paints in desired colors
2" (5 cm) paintbrush
Ruler and pencil
Awl
Nine water tubes with a lip **(B)**
Glue gun and glue
One bundle of colored raffia **(C)**
Scissors
Wire cutter

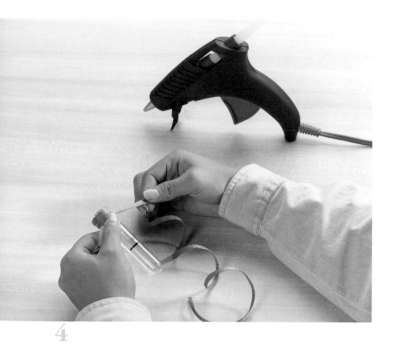

4

5 Cut nine 10" (25.5 cm) pieces of raffia. Insert the ends of one piece into the first set of holes on the front of the first canvas. Slip a water tube under the raffia and pull the raffia tight just under the lip of the tube. Tie the raffia tightly in a square knot on the back of the canvas. Repeat for the other two tubes on the canvas, and for the three tubes on each of the other two canvases. Touch a dot of glue to each knot.

6 Hang the canvases in a row in the numbered order, positioning them about 1" (2.5 cm) apart.

7 Cut the gerbera stems straight across, about 5½" (14 cm) long. Bend the blossoms forward. Touch a drop of glue to the end of each stem before placing it carefully into a tube.

Ardith suggests

Repetition of color and height is very soothing. But if that is not your aim, you can spark up the effect of this design by varying the heights of the flowers or using a mixture of flowers with different colors and textures.

Purse of Poppies

Poppies have a positive attitude. They are bright and uplifting, always turning their faces to the sun. Display this moss purse full of poppies wherever you need to add a day-brightener—at the front door, on a kitchen wall, or even in the office. A chicken wire form, hidden by a sheet of display moss, forms the purse pocket that holds the foam. Curly willow stems are shaped into an interesting handle but don't actually support the weight of the design.

Purse of Poppies

1 Bend in all the cut wires along the edges of the chicken wire to make it easier to handle.

2 Fold the chicken wire in half to 13" × 10" (33 × 25.5 cm), but don't crease the bottom. Stitch the sides together using 18" (46 cm) pieces of bindwire.

3 Cut several curly willow branches, and bend them into the shape of a handle. Secure the ends together with anchor tape. Tuck the branches down inside the purse and secure them along the sides of the chicken wire with anchor tape.

4 Cut two pieces of barked wire, about 2 yd. (1.85 m) long. Weave one of the wires through the chicken wire along the side of the purse,

Florals
Three stems fresh or dried curly willow
　　branches **(A)**
Handful of sheet moss
12 poppies, some with buds, in three
　　shades of a color **(B)**
Three stems fittonia leaves **(C)**

Tools and materials
Garden gloves
Green chicken wire, 13" × 20"
　　(33 × 51 cm)
Wire cutter
Green bindwire
Needle-nose pliers
Anchor tape, ¼" (6 mm) wide
4 yd. (3.7 m) barked wire
Display moss, 17" × 24" (43 × 61 cm) **(D)**
Glue pan or glue gun and glue
One block dry floral foam
Newspapers

from the opening to the bottom. Bend the end over the bottom wires of the purse, using needle-nose pliers. Then twist the free end of the wire randomly around the curly willow branches to look like another branch. At the opposite side of the purse, weave the wire down through the chicken wire and bend the end over the bottom wires. Repeat with the second piece of barked wire. This will support the sides of the purse and handle.

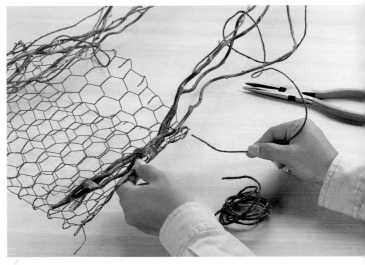

4

5 Lay the display moss facedown on the work surface. Lay the chicken wire form over it. The moss should extend 1" (2.5 cm) on the sides and 2" (5 cm) at the top. Fold the moss up over the front of the purse. Seal the sides of the moss with hot glue. Roll the moss to the inside at the purse opening, and glue it in place.

6 Insert the block of foam into the purse. Stuff the space around it with crumpled newspaper. Cover the foam and newspaper with sheet moss.

7 With the bindwire, make a wire hanger at each back top corner of the purse, following the directions on page 12. Hang the wreath over your work surface.

8 Cut the poppies into separate stems. Insert one stem into the foam with the flower high on the right; insert another stem with the flower low on the left. Insert the other flowers and buds at various heights, some close to the purse opening and others hanging over the front, forming a gentle flowing curve. Bend the stems into graceful curves and turn the flower faces toward the sun.

9 Insert the fittonia leaves close to the purse opening to fill any open spaces. Insert one or two thin willow branches draping down over the front of the purse.

6

Ardith suggests

Chicken wire can be vicious. Wear garden gloves to protect your hands from scratches.

Sea Monogram

Monogram letters are personalized wall designs. This project shows how to make a letter from foam-core board as a base for a floral design. This "C" is decorated with beach shells; use ones you've found on a beach or buy them at the craft store. The protea flowers and the Dendrobium orchids look like sea creatures. The flat-backed clear rocks look like big drops of water.

Sea Monogram

1   Choose a letter; enlarge it to the size you want. Trace the letter onto foam-core board, and cut it out using a craft knife and cutting board.

2   Lay the monogram on newspapers in a well-ventilated area. Spray the monogram with copper and glossy wood-tone color tool. Let it dry.

3   Make a hanger on the back near the top of the monogram with a chenille stem, following the directions on page 12. Make a second hanger lower on the monogram. Allow the glue to set.

4   Separate the seashells into groups by size. Attach the larger seashells to the monogram randomly, using hot glue.

Florals
One stem green/cream water plant **(A)**
One stem red/green water plant **(B)**
Three pincushion protea with foliage **(C)**
One stem Dendrobium orchid with five
    flowers and buds **(D)**

Tools and materials
Foam-core board, ¼" (6 mm) thick
Craft knife
Cutting board
Newspaper
Copper color tool
Glossy wood-tone color tool
Two chenille stems
Wire cutter
Glue pan or glue gun and glue
One pound assorted seashells
Scissors
Tack 2000 adhesive
Fine sand
20 light blue flat glass marbles

5   Cut the water plant stems apart into many small pieces. Glue half of the pieces in and around the shells.

6   Working over newspapers, lightly spray Tack 2000 over the entire monogram. Quickly sprinkle fine sand over it. Let it dry, and then shake off excess sand.

7   Cut the pincushion protea flowers from the stems. Glue them, evenly spaced, onto the monogram, using a generous amount of hot glue.

8   Add the remaining seashells and plant foliage to the monogram, filling in all the areas.

9   Glue the flat blue marbles here and there throughout the design to add sparkle and color. Use generous amounts of hot glue.

10   Cut the orchid flowers and buds from the stem, leaving 1" (2.5 cm) stems. Add them to the monogram, spacing them randomly and at various angles.

5

9

Ardith suggests

You can buy small amounts of very fine sand in several different colors at the craft store. Stick with the natural tone to make your monogram look like you found it at the bottom of the ocean, or give it a pastel tint by sprinkling it with colored sand.

Antiqued Basket of Roses

This quaint arrangement has the nostalgic appeal of an English rose garden. Antiqued metal wall baskets are popular items in craft stores and garden shops. The roses used for this design come as a mixed bush of flowers in several sizes and colors. Stems of lavender add texture, and crushed sheer ribbon loops and streamers add a little drama.

Antiqued Basket of Roses

1 Place patches of adhesive-back felt on the back of the metal basket in places that will touch the wall, to keep it from leaving marks.

2 Shape the floral foam so it fits into the basket and the top is level with the basket opening. Glue it into the basket.

3 Wrap the 24-gauge wire with floral tape (page 11). Form the ribbon into four small loops with long streamers. Wrap the center of the loops with the floral wire. Twist the wire ends together; cut them off 2" (5 cm) from the loops.

4 Insert the bow wires into the foam so the loops and streamers drape down over the left side of the basket.

Florals
One multicolored rose bush with
    12 flowers and foliage **(A)**
Half bush of lavender
    (about 18 stems) **(B)**

Tools and materials
Decorative metal wall basket
    with handle
Adhesive-back felt
One-third block dry floral foam
Glue pan or glue gun and glue
One 18" (46 cm), 24-gauge wire
Light green floral tape
2 yd. (1.85 m) wired ribbon,
    2¼" (6 cm) wide
Wire cutter
Ribbon scissors

5 Cut the rose bush apart into individual stems, leaving them as long as possible. Push the foliage up the stem to form collars around the flowers.

6 Insert the rose stems into the foam one at a time in a pleasing arrangement, similar to the photograph on page 76. Vary the heights and spacing. Bend and twist the stems so they face forward and up for a natural look. On stems that are left longer, push some of the foliage closer to the foam.

7 Insert the lavender stems throughout the design, radiating from the center.

5

Ardith suggests

Ribbon is a beautiful part of many floral designs, but often there's no need for a full bow, especially in a small arrangement. A few small loops and streamers can be enough to bring the texture and color of the ribbon into your wall design.

Woodland Cone

Here is a woodsy, naturalistic wall design that would be a great accent over a fireplace or hall table. Envision it on a brick wall. The twig cone, available at craft stores and floral design centers, is built around a strong wire form. Hang this design at eye level so the bird nest can be seen.

Woodland Cone

1. Hang the cone over your work surface at eye level. Line the inside of the cone with display moss, cutting and piecing the moss as needed.

2. Taper the corners of the foam block at one end and wedge the block down into the cone. The top of the foam should be level with or just below the lip of the cone.

3. Form the chicken wire over the top of the foam, bending the edges down into the cone. Twist one end of a 24-gauge wire around the wire support at the back left corner of the cone lip. Weave the wire through the chicken wire and around the cone lip to the front. Repeat on the right side with another wire. Bend the wire ends into the cone for safety.

4. Insert the end of the woody vine into the back right corner of the cone. Bend the vine out in

Florals
One woody vine permanent botanical with berries, 48" (122 cm) long **(A)**
One variegated ivy bush with nine stems **(B)**
Craft bird nest on a stem, 6" (15 cm) diameter **(C)**
Two orange lily stems, with five flowers **(D)**
Two stems green pineapple lily, each with two stems **(E)**
Two dried artichokes on stems **(F)**
Two permanent botanical curly willow stems, each with six branches **(G)**
One seneca vine with three stems **(H)**
Three stems dried salal **(I)**

Tools and materials
Twig wall cone with wire frame
Display moss, 24" (61 cm) square
One block dry floral foam
Green chicken wire, 12" × 9" (30.5 × 23 cm)
Three 18" (46 cm), 24-gauge wires
Bindwire
Wire cutter

3

6

a curve to the right of the cone, across the front to the left front corner, and down across the cone front to the lower right side. Shape the vine to look natural. Secure the vine to the support wires of the cone with bindwire at the front left corner and at the lower right side.

Insert the ivy bush into the right side of the cone, through the chicken wire and down between the foam and the cone. Trail the stems down the side and across the front of the cone.

Insert the stem of the nest into the foam so the nest rests over the woody stem. Spread the ivy around the nest base for a cozy appearance.

Cut the flowers from the lilies, leaving the flower stems as long as possible. Insert the longest stem into the foam with the flower high near the back left corner. Insert the second flower into the foam with the flower near the back right corner, slightly lower than the first flower. Insert the third stem with the flower 2" (5 cm) above the lip on the left side. Insert the fourth stem into the foam under the nest, with the flower facing left, resting over the vine. Insert the fifth flower low in the center, close to the left side of the nest.

Cut the stems from the pineapple lilies. Insert three stems high in the back left corner, at differ-

ent heights. Bend the stems naturally. Insert a fourth stem through the front of the cone, just below the lip, and turn the spike upward.

Insert one artichoke low in the design among the lilies on the left side. Insert the other artichoke low in the design in the center back.

Cut the stems from the permanent curly willow. Insert half of the stems, one at a time, into the back right corner and curve them out over the right side and down over the front. Curve some of them up over the nest. Insert the other stems, one at a time, into the left side and out in a wide curve to the bottom of the cone.

Cut the stems from the seneca vine. Insert them into the center front of the design, hanging down over the front of the cone.

Add salal and any other remaining foliage as needed to fill in and add texture.

Ardith suggests

Switch out the floral elements with the seasons to make this a year-round wall design.

Floralscape

This elegant, Asian-inspired design is like a three-dimensional painting. It is built on a large piece of artist canvas with a bamboo frame to set off the design. Out of the moss and rocks grow showy orchids on gracefully arching stems. These lifelike orchid plants are permanent botanicals with root systems, leathery leaves, and hairy stems.

Floralscape

1. Drill small holes through the 40" (102 cm) bamboo pieces, several inches from the ends. Lay the stretched canvas on the work surface with the short sides at the top and bottom. Center the bamboo pieces alongside the canvas frame. Attach the bamboo pieces to the long sides of the frame, using long, thin screws.

2. Center the two 28" (71 cm) bamboo pieces over the top and bottom edges of the canvas frame. Wire them tightly to the side bamboo pieces, using natural bindwire. Crisscross the wire over the front of the bamboo for a decorative effect. Apply hot glue along the top and bottom of the canvas to help hold the bamboo pieces in place.

Florals

Two bamboo stalks, ½" (1.3 cm) thick, 40" (102 cm) long **(A)**

Two bamboo stalks, ½" (1.3 cm) thick, 28" (71 cm) long

Two or three pieces river cane **(B)**

One green Dendrobium orchid plant with root system **(C)**

Three green/burgundy/brown Paphiopedilum orchid plants with root system **(D)**

15 assorted pods **(E)**

One orchid plant, foliage only, with root system **(F)**

Handful of light green reindeer moss **(G)**

Handful of dark green reindeer moss

Tools and materials

Gesso-primed stretched canvas, 24" × 36" (61 × 91.5 cm)

Drill with very small bit

Long thin screws

Screwdriver

Natural bindwire

Wire cutter

Glue pan or glue gun and glue

Display moss, 2" × 24" (5 × 61 cm)

Newspaper

Tack 2000 adhesive

Several assorted polished stones

Three moss rocks

3

6

Lay the strip of display moss facedown on newspaper in a well-ventilated area. Spray with Tack 2000 adhesive, and stick it across the canvas, 3" (7.5 cm) from the bottom.

Cut two river canes so one extends from the moss to 3" (7.5 cm) above the top of the canvas and the other is 7" (18 cm) shorter. Place them about 3" (7.5 cm) apart and 3" (7.5 cm) from the left side of the canvas. Cut three thin pieces of cane and cross them over the upright pieces at different angles. Secure them with criss-crossed bindwires, forming an armature. Secure the longer cane to the top bamboo with criss-crossed bindwire. Apply generous amounts of hot glue to the bottoms of the canes to hold them in place. Add dots of hot glue to the back of the shorter cane to hold it in place.

Shape the Dendrobium orchid to look natural. Glue the base of the plant to the moss strip, over the river canes. Secure the stem to the long cane in two places, using bindwire. Arch the stem toward the right, shaping the flowers naturally.

Shape the Paphiopedilum orchids. Place them in the design with the bases on the moss strip. Decide how high you want the flowers. If an orchid is too high, go deep inside the leaves to the base of the stem with your wire cutter, and

cut the stem. Then shorten it to the desired length, and glue the stem back in place.

Glue the bases of the plants to the moss strip at different heights. Curve the orchid stems gracefully so they stand away from the canvas surface, and glue the backs of the flowers to the canvas.

Glue the pods and stones along the base of the design over the moss strip. Begin with the larger ones and add smaller ones. Keep the root systems of the orchids free.

Shape the orchid foliage plant to look natural. Glue it at the base of the design near the center with the foliage opening toward the front rather than up.

Add the moss rocks and reindeer moss here and there along the base of the design. Shape the orchid roots over the rocks and moss to look natural.

Ardith suggests

Change the scene and create a different style by using different flowers, such as irises, tulips, or roses.

Floral Still Life

This is a miniaturized version of a grand floral arrangement, right down to the small silver urn. The scale is just right for a powder room or small bedroom. The mini-masterpiece spills dramatically out of a memory box frame.

Floral Still Life

1 Remove the glass from the frame. It won't be used for this project.

2 If the frame doesn't have hangers, attach a picture hanger to each back upper corner. Stand the frame on your work surface.

3 Cut the foam to fit the urn and come about ½" (1.3 cm) above the rim. Glue the foam into the urn.

4 Place a layered square of self-adhesive Velcro on the bottom of the urn base. Secure the urn to the bottom of the memory box frame, about one-third the distance from the left side. To make the urn stand without tipping, the base may have to overhang the edge of the frame. Place another layered square of

Florals
One stem ivy with small leaves **(A)**
One stem scabiosa with three flowers **(B)**
Two stems sweet peas **(C)**
One stem lady's mantle with flowers **(D)**
One bunch lavender **(E)**
One stem small berries **(F)**

Tools and materials
Memory box frame with 8" × 10"
   (20.5 × 25.5 cm) opening
Picture hangers, if not included with frame
One block dry floral foam
Metal urn, 4" (10 cm) high
Glue pan or glue gun and glue
Adhesive-back Velcro strip
Two or three small moss rocks

Velcro behind the urn to hold the rim to the back wall of the frame.

5 Glue the moss rocks here and there in the bottom of the frame.

6 Cut the ivy apart into pieces of different lengths. Insert the ivy into the foam, draping down around the urn and rocks.

7 Cut the scabiosa flowers from the stems, leaving the stems as long as possible. Insert the flowers into the foam with the largest flower on the right close to the urn rim, one flower extending straight up above the frame, and one straight out to the right. Turn the flower heads slightly forward and bend the stems to look natural.

8 Insert the sweet pea stems into the left side of the foam so the tallest flowers rise above and to the outer left of the frame. The rest of the sweet peas should be at different heights between the tall ones and the urn rim, with a couple draping down over the front of the urn and a couple to the left.

9 Cut the lady's mantle stems apart, leaving the flower stems as long as possible. Insert the lady's mantle so three of the flowers are midway between the urn rim and the tallest sweet peas, one on the left, one in the middle, and one on the right. Insert another lady's mantle with the flower extending toward the lower right corner of the frame.

10 Fill in the design with lavender stems and berry stems, keeping the lazy crescent shape from the top left to the bottom right.

4

7

Ardith suggests

If you have the wall space for a larger design, increase the scale of your floral still life with a bigger memory box and urn. To keep the design elements in proportion, choose florals with fuller flowers and broader foliage.

Wall Herb Garden

This simple but enchanting design features
a collection of garden herbs. Interesting
textures are found in the leaves, colors,
and stem structures. The permanent
botanicals I chose look so real, you have
to touch and smell them to discover the
difference. It costs a little more for such
high quality, but the plants look fabulous
and will last forever. This is a perfect wall
flower design for a kitchen.

Wall Herb Garden

1   Drill a small hole at each end of the back of the container, for hanging. Place adhesive-back cork circles on the back of the container in places that will touch the wall, to keep it from leaving marks.

2   Cut the foam into pieces to fit the pots and come ½" (1.3 cm) below the rims. Glue the foam into the pots.

3   Glue the squares of Styrofoam into the bottom of the container where the second and fourth pots will sit. Glue the pots into the container.

Florals
One small thyme plant **(A)**
One small rosemary plant **(B)**
One small cilantro plant **(C)**
One small mint plant **(D)**
One small sage plant **(E)**
Small amount of sheet moss

Tools and materials
Metal oblong container, 15" long × 3"
    high × 3½" wide (38 × 7.5 × 9 cm)
Drill and bits
Adhesive-back cork circles
One block dry floral foam
Five clay pots, 3" (7.5 cm) diameter
Glue pan or glue gun and glue
Two 2" (5 cm) squares Styrofoam,
    ¾" (2 cm) thick
2 yd. (1.85 m) narrow wire-edge ribbon
Wire cutter

4   Cut the herb plants into separate stems. Insert the stems of one variety into each pot in a natural arrangement. Cover any visible foam with pieces of moss.

5   Wrap the ribbon around the container and tie it in a simple bow on the left side of the front. Trim and shape the tails.

4

Ardith suggests

If you don't want to damage your container by gluing Styrofoam and clay pots into it, cover the bottom with duct tape first. When you want to change the design, simply remove the duct tape and you'll have a clean surface.

Sitting Pretty

A shelf made from a weathered chair back brings a homey, comfortable feeling to any space. Country-style and casual, this simple arrangement goes together quickly. With each new season, you can easily change the flowers on the shelf. Look for a shelf like this at craft stores, floral shops, and home décor stores.

Sitting Pretty

1

1. Cut the foam into three pieces to fit the pots and come ½" (1.3 cm) below the rims. Glue the foam into the pots.

2. Separate the flower and grass stems of the daisy bush. Insert them into the foam in one pot in a natural arrangement. Cover any visible foam with pieces of moss.

3. Separate the flower and grass stems of the ranunculus bush. Set aside a few flowers and buds. Insert the other stem into the foam in another pot in a natural arrangement. Cover any visible foam with pieces of moss.

4. Separate the stems of the pilea plant. There will be several different lengths. Insert the shorter stems into the center of the third pot. Insert

Florals
One daisy bush with grass **(A)**
One small ranunculus bush with grass **(B)**
One trailing cream-frosted pilea plant **(C)**
One small grapevine wreath **(D)**

Tools and materials
One block dry floral foam
Three matching decorative pots,
    each one-third the width of the shelf
Glue pan or glue gun and glue
Wire cutter
Small amount of sheet moss
2 yd. (1.85 m) each of narrow ribbons
    in three colors
Ribbon scissors
Chair shelf
Drill and screws

longer stems around the outer edges. Cover any visible foam with pieces of moss.

5 Casually twist the ribbons around the wreath and tie them together at the bottom, leaving long streamers. Glue the reserved ranunculus flowers and buds here and there on the wreath.

6 Drill holes into the bottom of the shelf and up into the thickest back posts. Insert screws for added support. Hang the shelf.

7 Place the pots on the shelf with the pilea plant in the center. Trail some of the longer stems around the flowering pots and up onto the chair back for a natural look. Hang the wreath on the chair post opposite the ranunculus pot.

6

Ardith suggests

I bought my chair-shelf ready-made, but you could make one from an old wooden chair with a flat seat and fairly straight back. Remove the legs and saw off the seat at the desired depth. Attach a heavy-duty picture hanger to the center back. Hang the shelf and move the bottom out from the wall until the shelf is level. Attach angle irons to the underside of the shelf to hold it level and screw them to the wall for support.

Fall Welcome

Hang this quick and easy fall decoration on or alongside the front door to welcome visitors with the colors and textures of the season. Sunflowers and fall leaves make it suitable for late summer into autumn. Look for a child-size bamboo rake at the hardware store or garden center.

Fall Welcome

1 Make a hanger with a chenille stem on the rake handle at the base of the teeth. Wind the autumn ivy garland around the rake handle, securing it at the top and bottom with hot glue.

2 From the raffia ribbon, make a bow with several loops, leaving streamers 24" and 18" (61 and 46 cm) long. Wire the center of the bow with a chenille stem. Then wire the bow to the rake handle, at the base of the teeth.

3 Drape the streamers down the rake handle and around the ivy garland. Glue them in a few spots to the handle. Trim the ends at an angle.

Florals
One grape ivy garland in autumn colors, 1 yd. (0.92 m) long **(A)**
Two stems autumn berries **(B)**
Three small sunflowers **(C)**
One stem purple safflower with five flowers **(D)**
One stem glycerized autumn leaves **(E)**

Tools and materials
Child-size leaf rake
Two green chenille stems
Glue gun and glue
3 yd. (2.75 m) raffia ribbon, 3" (7.5 cm) wide
Ribbon scissors

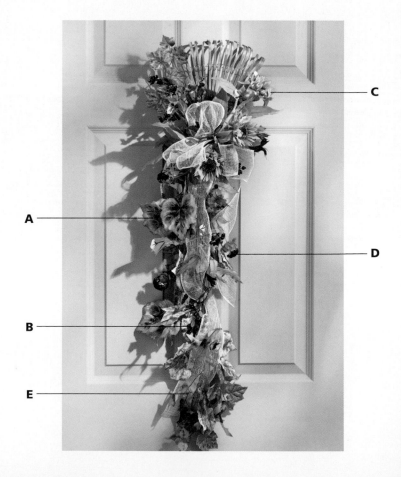

2

4 Intertwine the berry stems into the design. Glue the stem ends into the center of the bow.

5 Cut the sunflowers, leaving 3" (7.5 cm) stems. Glue one in the center of the bow, facing down. Glue the second sunflower behind the bow facing up to the right. Glue the third sunflower higher to the right, alongside the rake teeth.

6 Cut the safflowers from the main branch, leaving the stems as long as possible. Glue them into the design here and there along the left side, down the handle, and near the bow.

7 Glue glycerized leaves here and there throughout the design, some in a cluster near the bow, others on the handle and ribbon.

Ardith suggests

You could also design a floral arrangement around another child-size garden tool, like a small shovel. To keep the tool from scratching the wall or door, glue patches of felt to areas of the tool that touch the surface.

Autumn Border

This attractive wall accent uses a section of decorative metal garden edging for a base. It is a horizontal design that would work well over a headboard, fireplace, or buffet. For a country look, you could use a section of picket fence edging.

Autumn Border

1. Hang the metal edging over your work surface. Lay a birch branch over the bottom of the edging, with the smaller branches extending to the left. Secure the branch to the edging with bindwire. Lay a second branch in the opposite direction; secure with bindwire.

2. Bend the gooseberry stem at the point where the berries and foliage begin. Twist the bare stem around the left side of the edging and weave it through the bottom of the edging. Wire it to the birch branches and edging with bindwire. Shape the free end of the branch naturally across the front of the design, twisting it around the branches here and there to hold it in place.

3. Glue the nest into the branches in the left third of the design.

4. Cut 3" (7.5 cm) from the stem of one teasel seed spray, and weave the stem through the

Florals
Two natural birch branches, each 24"
 (61 cm) long **(A)**
One autumn gooseberry branch with
 foliage, berries, and blossoms **(B)**
Two sprays teasel seed, 24" (61 cm)
 long **(C)**
Two sprays burgundy mini carnations,
 each with four flowers **(D)**
One dried olive-green oak branch cut
 into six parts **(E)**
One bunch dried bear grass **(F)**
One bird nest **(G)**

Tools and materials
One section metal garden edging,
 18" × 20" (46 × 51 cm)
Green bindwire
Glue pan or gun and glue
Anchor tape, ¼" (6 mm) wide

1

7

edging on the right side, so the seed heads are even with the top of the edging. Cut the second spray shorter and glue it in front of the first one.

Cut 6" (15 cm) from one carnation spray. Glue it into the center of the design, behind the branches. Cut the second spray into separate stems and glue them in place as if growing from the first spray.

Insert the olive oak pieces into the design here and there to add depth and texture.

Wrap the base of the bear grass bundle tightly with anchor tape. Wrap the bundle two more times, spacing the anchor tape wraps 6" (15 cm) apart. Cut the bundle into three pieces, cutting under the second and third tape wraps. Cut the bundles flat and a bit irregular, to resemble cut summer grass. Dip the taped ends in hot glue. Then place all three bundles into the design on the far left.

Ardith suggests

You can leave the metal border on the wall and change the florals with the seasons. In the spring, put tiny eggs in the nest; in the summer, a bird.

Copper
Crescent

Gold, silver, and copper have become very popular in Christmas decorations. This gorgeous evergreen crescent just glows. It features copper poinsettias and ribbon accents. The design goes together quickly on a purchased base with a hanger. In no time at all, you'll have an impressive, glimmering holiday design to hang on the wall above a door or over a mantel.

Copper Crescent

1. Wrap the wires with floral tape (page 11) and cut each into four equal pieces. Bend the wires into U shapes and set them aside.

2. Lay the magnolia garland over the crescent. Dip the ends of a bent wire from step 1 into the glue. Straddle a garland stem with the wire and insert the wire ends into the wreath base. Repeat along the length of the crescent, securing the garland to the base and covering all the areas that will be seen. Save one wire for the bow.

3. Hang the crescent over your work surface. Make a generous bow with 18" (46 cm) streamers, using 3 yd. (2.75 m) of ribbon. Wire the center with 22-gauge wire, and twist the wire ends together. Insert the bow into the crescent at the center front.

4. Cut the poinsettias from the stems, leaving 3" (7.5 cm) stems with sharply angled points. Insert one into the left end of the crescent, draping

Florals

One green/brown magnolia garland,
   3 ft. (0.92 m) long **(A)**
Three stems large copper poinsettias **(B)**
Two copper leaf stems, each with five
   leaves **(C)**
Two stems copper-tinted evergreens,
   each with five branches **(D)**

Tools and materials

Four 18" (46 cm), 22-gauge wires
Green floral tape
Wire cutter
Ready-to-use green-flocked
   Styrofoam crescent
Glue pan or glue gun and glue
6 yd. (5.5 m) double-face wire-edge
   ribbon, 2¼" (56 mm) wide
Ribbon scissors
12 small gold papier-mâché stars
3 yd. (2.75 m) copper bead garland

2

7

over the end; insert the second one halfway between the center and the left end, facing up and left; insert the third one halfway between the center and the right end, facing forward.

Cut the copper leaf stems into three parts each; arrange the leaves to look natural. Insert them deep into the crescent around the poinsettias.

Cut the remaining ribbon into three equal pieces to make ribbon roses. Fold one piece in half lengthwise. Gently pull out the ribbon wires a few inches at one end. Fold that end over diagonally and wrap the bottom tightly with the wires to form a rose base.

Gather the remaining ribbon length along the ribbon wires to about 18" (46 cm), pulling the wires from the opposite end. Wrap the gathered edge around the rose base, wrapping each layer slightly wider than the previous one. Fold the ribbon end down and catch it under the last layer. Wrap the ribbon wires tightly around the base to secure.

Repeat steps 6 and 7 to make three roses. Glue one rose next to the second poinsettia from the left; glue another rose at the top center; glue the third rose at the far right end of the crescent.

Cut the stems of copper-tinted evergreens into three pieces each. Insert them equally spaced into the crescent, facing away from the center.

Glue the gold stars to the crescent, randomly spaced.

Drape the bead garland through the crescent, beginning on the left, winding it among the flowers and leaves to the far right and back again. Touch with glue here and there to keep it in place.

Ardith suggests

There are faux florals and ribbons in all metallic finishes—bright silver, pewter, bright gold, antique gold, copper, and combinations of metallics. If you don't find what you like, you can tint flowers and foliage with special spray paints and dyes designed for florals.

About the Author

Ardith Beveridge, AIFD, AAF, PFCI, is a master floral designer, educator, and judge. She is the director of education and instructor for the Koehler & Dramm Institute of Floristry. She also co-owns a floral design video production company, Floral Communications Group Inc., and is the instructor in

Photo: John S. Maciejny

the company's twelve series of do-it-yourself videos. Ardith's creativity and enthusiasm have captivated audiences in programs and workshops across the country and internationally. By special invitation, Ardith has designed for presidential inaugurations and other prestigious national and international events. She also appears regularly on television. Her professional certifications include the American Institute of Floral Designers, American Academy of Floriculture, Professional Floral Communicators International, Society of Floristry LTD (England), and the Canadian Academy of Floral Arts. She is a design education specialist for Teleflora wire service, a Smithers Osasis design director, and a master designer for FTD. In 2005, Ardith was inducted into the South Dakota Florist's Association Hall of Fame.